Small Talk:

Master the Art of Small Talk Easily and Effectively with These 10 Easy Steps.

Jessica Forrest

Table of Contents

Introduction

Thank you for purchasing *Small Talk: Master the Art of Small Talk Easily and Effectively with These 10 Easy Steps*. Being able to hold a natural, prolonged conversation is a skill that is valuable in virtually every facet of life. Luckily, making small talk becomes easier over time which is why the following chapters will lead you through the process before suggesting you start practicing with strangers before moving on to making small talk at work and then while on a date.

Each of the following chapters can be thought of as a step to ensuring that you can strike up a conversation with anyone and speak for hours about nothing at all. To do so you simply need to know the differences between good and bad conversation, how to listen, how to work around awkward silences and how to begin and end a conversation with ease. Your ability to converse will only improve with dedication, but if you put in the effort you will find the reward well worth it.

There are plenty of books on this subject on the market, thanks again for choosing this one! Every effort was made to ensure it is full of as much useful information as possible, please enjoy!

Chapter 1: The Basics of Good Conversation

While most people are comfortable making conversation with friends and family, some people can easily go beyond this boundary and talk to anyone about anything. If this type of interaction seems unfathomable to you, there are numerous things that you can do to make conversing with anyone at any time, not only conceivable but manageable, and maybe, with practice, something that is easy and fun to do. While starting a conversation is covered in chapter 5, you will find that you are more prepared to do so, if you spend some time considering the following basic things every good conversation has in common first.

Make it clear you care about what the other person is saying: You will be surprised how much easier it is to talk to a complete stranger if you use the first part of the conversation to make it clear that you care about what the other person is saying.

In general, people are more likely to open up and consider you interesting if you ask them plenty of questions as this shows you are interested in learning new things. This will also make the other person more relaxed and more likely to share an even more in depth conversation. Always be sure to maintain an appropriate amount of eye contact, at least 50 percent of the time while speaking and at least 70 percent of the time while listening as well as listening actively as described in chapter 3.

Balance the conversation:

It is important to ensure than any conversation you get into is one that has the right mix of back and forth between you and the other person. If you are shy by nature, then the best way to get the proper flow is to ask a few open ended questions that you think will give the other person plenty to talk about. After you have asked them to elaborate on their opinions once or twice you should feel more comfortable about jumping in. Having a balanced conversation is important because otherwise the other person is likely going to feel as though they are being interrogated and begin to feel uncomfortable, at worst; or, at best, simply eventually get bored and move on. Everyone likes talking about themselves; most people don't enjoy doing so indefinitely.

If you find yourself in a situation where nerves cause you to either talk too much or to freeze up and not talk enough. In either situation it is important to take a moment to breathe and focus before smiling in a way that says you are slightly, but not seriously, embarrassed by your actions before redirecting the conversation as appropriate, ideally by choosing a new conversation topic related to the reason you and the other person are both in the same place at the same time. If this happens it is important to not focus on it once it has passed, people like other people who acknowledge their flaws without apologizing profusely for them. As long as you downplay the awkward moment you will be fine.

Always have something to say:

If you traditionally have a hard time coming up with conversation topics this might be because you aren't keeping up on the types of general things that people talk about. Know your audience and start keeping abreast of the topics that you know they are interested in. If you are looking to be more conversational in general, they consider keeping tabs on current cultural trends, music or technological or scientific discoveries. Avoid talking about politics unless you are confident you share the same views as the other person.

Chapter 2: The Basics of Bad Conversation

Once you have a better idea of what good conversation entails, the next thing you are going to want to do is avoid the following conversation killers if you want the other person to stick around long enough to help you practice steps 3-10.

Parroting:

If you and another person are having a conversation, but instead of a back and forth interplay between individuals, all you are doing is repeating their opinions while adding little else to the conversation, then unfortunately, it isn't really a conversation. This is parroting and while some people won't get bored with this type of non-conversation, they likely aren't the ones you really want to talk to anyway. Even if you share the same opinions as the person you are speaking with, it is important to always make an effort to add something substantive to the conversation if you want the other person to come away from the conversation with an opinion on your opinions.

Emotionless conversation:

Regardless of how interesting your stories or perspective on current events might be, if you don't share them in the right way then no one will be able to maintain their interest long enough to hear the stories or agree/disagree with your opinions. Memorable conversation is alive with emotion and emphasis that travels between everyone involved in it. Bad conversation, on the other hand can only ever limp along, waiting to be put out of its misery. In order to convey more emotion, it may be helpful to think of your voice like the track of a roller coaster. Instead of keeping things flat and boring, mix it up with vocal variations that are appropriate for the conversation you are having. Don't forget to emphasize with hand motions as well as a way to sell especially emphatic moments.

Predictable conversation:

If you are the type of person who, in the middle of the conversation, always excuses yourself by saying exactly where you are going, or always uses the space of a conversation as simply a time for little more than a literal transmission of data between parties then the people you are speaking with may consider you a predictable, and therefore boring, conversationalist. If you feel as though the conversations you are having are too literal, then you may find success by being more playful. Joke around, make off the wall remarks on occasion, try and mix things up with a little frivolity and you should notice other people becoming more engaged with what you are saying.

Narcissistic conversation:

Even if what you are saying is said in a way that is interesting, if all you ever talk about is yourself, then people will be naturally turned off from speaking with you. Those who are unsure of how to proceed conversationally often fall into the trap of talking about themselves, or not talking enough and both are equally as bad. Branch out in terms of conversation topics and only talk about yourself if the story has a funny ending or is relevant to the current conversation.

Sentence hijacking:

While in a conversation, if the other person is speaking and you finish their sentence for them then you have just become a conversation hijacker. Except in especially familiar situations or those that are about coming to a mutual consensus, this is typically considered disrespectful to the person who was speaking. What's worse, if you get it wrong then you are being disrespectful as well as indicating that what you said is more important than what the actual conversation was about. This then causes the conversation to become disjointed and thrown off the flow in a way that can be difficult to recover from.

Instead of assuming that you know what the other person is going to say, come up with a question to further determine their specifics before moving forward. If you are in a habit of finishing other people's sentences, the best way to break yourself of that habit is by simply being aware of it as this should likely stop you from speaking before you have the time to censor yourself. Don't beat yourself up if it doesn't correct the problem all at once, it will get easier with practice.

Chapter 3: Learn to Listen

When you are in a conversation, it is just as important to make the other person feel as though you are listening as it is to be actively engaged in whatever it is they are saying. It is important to make an effort to listen with all of your senses, and make it clear to the other person that you really comprehend whatever it is they are talking about. This is what is known as active listening and perfecting the techniques below will help ensure your body is always on message.

Physical signs of listening

Smile:

Smiling at the right times while you are listening says that you appreciate what the other person is saying, or agree broadly with the topic being discussed or the specific information being conveyed. When added to a simple head nod, a smile is a way to say that you understand what is being asked of you and you will go ahead and do it.

Eye contact:

Depending on how many people you are speaking to and what else is going on around the conversation, making eye contact is a great way for the other party to know that you are listening to what they are saying. Ensure you maintain enough eye contact to show you are interested while not keeping it so intently that it is seen as inappropriate.

Posture:

The posture you use while listening can say a lot about your thoughts on the information in the conversation being conveyed. If you are actively listening, you will want to make it a point of leaning towards the person who is speaking. You will want to add to this by either resting your head on your hand while staring at the speaker or tilt your head to the side slightly to indicate you are listening.

Mirroring:

Mirroring the actions and mannerisms of the person you are listening to is a subconscious way of letting them know that you both are on the same page. This should look natural, however, as being noticed trying to mimic certain expressions will make it appear that you are not listening at all. Alternatively, if you start mimicking the other person and then start doing your own gestures or expressions and see them mimic you, you will know you have control of the conversation.

Don't appear distracted:

Even if you are listening intently, doing things like looking at your phone, fidgeting, or nitpicking your appearance will all give the speaker the assumption of the opposite. Give the person you are listening to your full attention and they will assume you are listening more competently as a result.

Remember key points:

If you want to show the other person that you were really listening, one of the best ways to do so is to remember key pieces of information about a conversation you had previously. Don't worry about remembering the details, the gist of the conversation will be enough to cause them to react favorably to your effort.

Ask questions:

While many people who feel awkward in conversation may believe that asking questions is a good way to imply you weren't paying attention; in reality, it is a great way to show you value what the other person is saying so much that you want to ensure you get it right. The questions you are asking should appear as though they are digging deeper on the topic, not simply rehashing what has already been said.

Clarification:

Much like with asking questions, asking for clarification on what has been said, assuming the details have not already been clarified is a great way to make it clear to the other person that you are definitely invested in what they have to say. It is important to ask for clarification all at once, however, as breaking it up can cause the conversation to feel stilted an unnatural.

Summarization:

At the end of the conversation, a good way to make it clear you were listening the entire time is to summarize the conversation as discussed to ensure that you and the speaker were on the same page. Again, this indicates you are going to put the conversation into action, not that you weren't paying attention.

Chapter 4: Dealing with Awkward Silences

No matter how well any conversation is going, there are always going to be moments when everyone involved runs out of things to say at the same time. This is perfectly natural, however, and can be easily overcome if you don't blow them out of proportion and instead try the various suggestions described below.

Consider why the silence occurred:

Depending on the nature of the conversation that you are having, the fact that there is a silence during the conversation might not even be awkward. If you and the other person are talking while also doing another task, then it might simply be a function of the nature of the conversation that lead to the silence. Additionally, some people might not even like small talk and instead feel more comfortable during a silence. Consider how the other person seems to be responding to the silence before assuming that it is automatically somehow your fault.

Don't overemphasize the silence:

Depending on the reason the silence occurred, it is important to not get so anxious about it that you do something that ultimately makes it worse instead of better. There is always a chance that the other person hasn't considered the silence awkward and calling attention to it will only make the situation worse instead of better. Instead of worrying about it, put your mind to work coming up with a way to break the silence.

Consider alternative topics of conversation:

If your conversation has hit a lull, take a few moments to consider continuing the current train of thought before instead considering where to move the conversation next.

Start by thinking about previous conversation threads that were put aside and see if you can ask a related question to get things moving again in the right direction. If nothing jumps out at you right away, then it will be time to consider a new topic of conversation. The best place to start is with something related to the reason you are both in the same place at the same time or why you started talking in the first place. Remember, if the silence is awkward, then it is likely that the other party will be grateful for a new topic of conversation so it is important to not be afraid to throw one out there.

Comment on it:

While it won't always be appropriate to comment on the silence, it will be the right choice on occasion. This is usually a valid conversation approach if the conversation died down due to a very specific reason. You can downplay the silence if it is because the other person didn't have something to say to a question you asked, make a joke about the reason for a silence, or even comment on it as a way to break the tension. Whatever option you go with, it is important that you have a new direction to take the conversation in afterwards if you don't want to end up right where you started.

Know when to be verbose:

Sometimes awkward silences occur because the other person has said something that they expected you to comment on at length and you instead answered with a one-word response. Keeping a conversation going is a 2-person job, and this sometimes means talking at length about something that you otherwise aren't all that keen to discuss. If you find yourself in this situation, keep up the back and forth until you manage to find a way to move the conversation to a more pleasant topic.

Utilize the silence:

If you were planning on exiting a conversation relatively soon anyway, there are few better times to make your exit than when a silence naturally occurs. Sometimes silences occur because there is nothing left to say and if you don't take the exit when it is presented you and the other person will end up stuck in an awkward post-conversation conversation where nothing interesting will be said for a few minutes until the silence sets in once more. Know when to get out on a high note and don't feel overly-committed to any conversation, especially with a stranger.

Chapter 5:

Starting a Conversation

Now that you have learned what can turn a conversation from neutral to either good or bad, it is time to start thinking about the best way to start a conversation with a stranger regardless of the time or the place. Before you get started it is important to understand that making conversation is a skill which means it will get easier with practice, but also that it will *only* get easier with practice. While you are bound to make a few mistakes while you are getting the hang of it, just keep in mind that the next time will always be easier.

Start with a compliment:

One of the easiest ways to start a conversation with a stranger is by complimenting them on either an aspect of their appearance or something that they are currently doing. This will automatically make them more inclined to talk to you as complimenting someone is one of the best ways to get their attention, especially if you follow it up with a question that allows them to talk about themselves in detail. Remember, everyone likes a compliment, and if you think something is extra special about a person today, odds are it didn't happen by accident and the other person put time and effort into standing out in that way. Noticing this validates their choices and will automatically make you more likeable in their eyes.

Start by talking about something they are obviously interested in:

If you are trying to make conversation with someone but don't know where to start, a good choice is to simply be observant and lead with something that indicates you know something about that apparent hobby or interest or are otherwise curious to know more. This is a great way to break the ice because it can give you plenty to talk about while at the same time helping you learn more about the other person in the process. Remember to be an active listener in this scenario for the best results.

Lead with something about your surroundings:

It doesn't matter where you are; the fact that you and the other person are both in the same place at the same time automatically means you have something in common. What's more, depending on where you currently are, there are numerous other similarities that can naturally shine through based on the limiting factors leading people to the spot. Additionally, your current surroundings are something that everyone is going to have an opinion on if you phrase it properly which makes it less likely that you will get only a few word answer in response, even if the other person wasn't previously interested in talking.

Be sure to actively listen as the other person speaks and be on the lookout for additional follow up topics to discuss when the conversation begins to lull.

Work to find common ground:

Depending on the scenario that finds you and the other person together, a good way to find a reliable conversation topic is to ask questions in hope of finding solid conversational ground. This means questions about hobbies, pop culture, music, books and the like are all fertile ground as all it takes is one similar interest to turn the exploratory conversation into a real conversation. If you do a bit of prospective probing, you never know what similarities you might find.

SOFTEN the other person up:

Regardless of what approach you take, there are some nonverbal techniques you will also want to consider when conversing with someone new for the first time. You want to start by Smiling at the other person to show that you are approachable and agreeable in general. Next, you are going to want to greet them with an Open posture to show that you are open to new ideas. Then you are going to want to lean forward to ensure they know you are interested in the conversation. After that you will want to initiate physical Touch by shaking hands which will automatically make the other person think more highly of you. Then you will to ensure you make appropriate eye contact. Finally, you will want to nod along with the other person which will keep them naturally talking longer.

Chapter 6: Ending a Conversation

When it comes to ending a conversation properly, the most important thing to remember is that you always need to have a clear agenda when doing so. If you don't know what you are going to do directly after you have made an effective exit from the conversation, then that exit will be wasted and instead the other person will be left with the, presumably correct, assumption that you simply did not care for their company. Knowing what you are going to do next, will also make it easier for you to motivate yourself into action when getting out the conversation might seem difficult or awkward. Remember, practice makes perfect!

Start by finding the right moment to bow out gracefully:

The first step to exiting a conversation properly is to choose the right moment to do so. Obviously, this won't be when the current topic of conversation is only being started or at any point while the other person is speaking or about to speak. When the conversation next begins to stall, instead of finding a new topic to discuss, you can begin by saying something like, "Okay," now this could either by an invitation for more conversation or ending it so it is likely the other person will repeat it back questioningly. With this opening you are then going to move on to the next step.

Return to the beginning:

Next, if the conversation started because of a specific question you asked, and that topic is what you were truly interested in, then bringing the conversation back around to that topic is a good way to get out gracefully. Use whatever the topic is as a starter and then make it clear that you will take what the other person said on the matter to heart to leave a lasting impression. This is a great way to end a conversation with a colleague (see chapter 10) as these conversations generally start with a specific request in mind and returning to it is a great way to show you were paying attention as well.

Finish with the right exit line:

Once you have brought things full circle, you are going to want to cite a reason that you are leaving and say your goodbyes. The first thing you will want to remember in this situation is to be as honest as possible, without being rude. In addition to being the easiest way of getting out of the conversation it prevents you from having to remember an elaborate lie later on.

Additionally, it is important to place the emphasis on what you need to do next as this will make the other person feel as though they are not the reason you are leaving. Actions that have time sensitive components are always the best choice as it takes the matter out of your hands completely. Blaming a third party is also a reliable strategy. Alternatively, if you were the one who initiated the conversation then you can bring it to an end then you want to bring the word "just" into play. For example, "Well, I just wanted to check and make sure that..." This makes it clear that you had a clear agenda and are interested in moving on.

If the other party initiated the conversation to discuss something in particular, you can easily get out of the conversation by asking them if there was anything else you could help with, followed by a reason you are being so direct. It is important to not use this closer until you then have something else to do, otherwise it can seem cold.

If the above options aren't appropriate, there are a few generic closers you can always try to help the other person realize the conversation is at an end. It is important to always use past tense language in this scenario to keep the focus where it needs to be. Phrases like "Anyway, it was great to," compress everything you are hoping to convey into a few simple syllables. Making it clear you value the other person's time is also a good choice, as in implying that you will let them get back to whatever it is they were doing.

Chapter 7: Fake It Until You Make It

If you find that despite your best efforts, you can't muster up the courage to talk to strangers just to make it easier for you to talk to strangers in the near and distant future; there is one simple thing that you can do to make the entire practicing process much more manageable. All you need to do if you find yourself in this situation is to fake it until you make it. Specifically, you are going to want to fake having the confidence level that you wish you had and introduce yourself to strangers as if it was something that you did all of the time.

While this might still sound impossible, consider the fact that if you interact with another person in a confident way, even if you are just pretending to be confident, the other person is never going to know the difference unless you stop pretending. When it comes to confidence, it doesn't matter how confident you are on the inside, the end result for everyone else is always going to be the same. What's more, if you pretend to be confident for long enough, something great will happen, you won't have to pretend anymore and the confidence will be real. If this all sounds like a tall tale, give it a try, you will be surprised by the results.

Find a confidence role model:

When it comes to acting like you are confident, it is as easy as taking the time to consider the person who you consider to be more self-confident than anyone else you know. With a clear image in your mind you are going to want to then ask yourself how the person in question would approach the conversation you are about to have. The more specific you can be when it comes to actions and mannerisms the better; this means things like body language, patterns of speech and conversational habits. Put yourself into your role model's headspace as completely as possible and then do what they would do.

Approach with purpose:

Those with an appropriate level of self-confidence tend to walk everywhere they go with a purpose. When you approach someone new, this means you are going to want to do so with your head held back and your shoulders squared. If you present yourself while slumped over and slouching you are telling the other person that you do not have confidence in yourself and that they should not either. You will also want to walk a little more quickly than normal to indicate that you are someone who knows where they need to be.

Be complementary:

Self-confident individuals are able to more easily see the good in those around them because they are familiar with what's great about them as well. This means that approaching confidently and then following that up by starting a conversation with a complement and a follow up question is a one-two punch that virtually guarantees the other person will remember you as someone who is confident in themselves and their abilities.

Consider how starting a conversation makes you seem:

Self-confident individuals are typically considered more friendly and outgoing than their peers. As such, simply by being the one to make first contact with a stranger, automatically makes them perceive you as being more confident than they are. This knowledge should then make it even easier for you to act self-confident as you are acting to an audience that has already been convinced. Taking the time to always introduce yourself to people you haven't met before, even if you don't then initiate conversation will let them know that you know you are a person with value who deserves respect.

Speak with confidence:

When you do speak, it is important to always have a clear idea of what information you want to convey and how you are going to go about conveying it. This will make easier for you to avoid words that the mind often inserts while it is thinking such as "like" or "uh". Additionally you will want to ensure that you are keeping a steady speaking pace as speaking too quickly will imply that you are nervous about the interaction, undermining your confident façade.

Chapter 8: Conversing with Strangers

When it comes to making conversation, starting one up with a stranger that you have no context for interacting with is definitely the hardest hurdle to overcome. While these circumstances can certainly be anxiety inducing, it is important to understand that they also have the least real world stakes because there is nothing that says you ever have to see the other person again if it ends up going poorly and you feel embarrassed. As such, it is recommended conversing with strangers until you are comfortable doing so before moving on to those you would feel worse being embarrassed by. Remember, practice makes perfect.

It is important to not push yourself to talk to too many strangers, too quickly, while at the same time not putting it off indefinitely so that you continue to make progress. Start slow, but remember to push yourself if you ever hope to make talking to strangers' second nature. While it might be difficult, the longer you push yourself beyond your comfort zone, the larger your comfort zone will be.

Be approachable:

When you are out in the world, you will find it naturally easier to get into conversations with strangers if you are looking at the world around you and making eye contact with the people you pass instead of looking down at your feet or at your phone.

Smile along with the eye contact, this will help you to not only determine viable conversation partners based on who does the same, but will help you to get in the habit of doing it often while talking to others. You will also want to ensure that your body language is open which means walking with your hands at your sides and not holding anything in front of you. Avoid crossing your arms as this indicates you are closed off and not interested in conversation.

Start small:

Assuming there is nothing going on in the area that warrants commenting on, then you are going to want to open with what is known as a cold-approach which means you are going to want to start small. Small conversation starters are things like asking for the time or asking for a small favor (watch a bag, plug in a USB charger). Your goal should be something small enough to be nominal but should take long enough to develop slightly more of a personal interaction. An open ended question that gives you a reason to elaborate on what you are asking for is ideal.

Introductions:

When the cold-approach succeeds, the next thing you are going to want to do is introduce yourself. Always offer your hand and say your own name and never ask for the other person's name, especially if they don't give it after you introduce yourself. If the other person doesn't give their name in return, odds are they aren't interested in making conversation.

Meat of the conversation:

It is at this point that you are going to want to start in on either open ended questions or asking for an explanation of something, depending on the specifics around the person you are speaking with. Your goal should be to find points of connection and nurture them will follow up questions. As soon as you can find something that you relate to, you will stop being strangers and start being acquaintances joined by that related interest.

This doesn't mean you need to do nothing but agree with the other person, however, as it is important to be yourself, especially if you hope to speak with the stranger again in the future. As long as you remain polite it is perfectly fine to have a disagreement as it can lead to lively conversation in its own right. Avoid extremely personal topics, however, as you want the discourse to remain friendly, not turn biting.

Body language is the key during any argument, keep your body language open and remember to smile. Likewise, watch for the other person's body language to change from open to closed as this is a good sign that they are no longer arguing in fun. Closed body language includes things like crossed arms or legs, increasing the distance between the two of you and pointing their body away from yours.

Chapter 9: Conversing with Colleagues

Whether you are just starting out at a new job or are simply looking for a way to connect more with your current co-workers who you can't seem to ingratiate yourself too, finding the right things to talk about at work can be tricky. This chapter lists ideas for both, though often you will find that a mix and match approach tends to work best.

New job

When you start a new job, the biggest hurdle to get over is likely going to be introducing yourself. This will certainly not get any easier over time, which is why it is best to introduce yourself to everyone you meet, the first time that you meet them. Remember always do your best to make a great first impression and be open to any conversation that results from your introduction. It is important to not be disappointed if everyone you speak with isn't interested in an in-depth conversation, it is an office after all.

Open by commenting on how the week is going:

If business is booming or simply creeping along, there is always something going on that warrants a conversation. After opening with a comment about the state of things, be sure to quickly segue into what the colleague thinks about the issue in relation to their experience with the company. From there you can start digging a little deeper by asking for some more personal details which you will want to file away for later to show that you are a good listener and care about your coworkers.

Find out how long they have been with the company:

When you ask someone how long they have been with the company; you are giving them carte blanche to tell you everything they think about your new workplace which means that finding someone who has been with the company for several years can be invaluable when it comes to getting the lay of the land. What's more, as long as the conversation goes well, you can likely count on that person to introduce you to everyone else around the office, saving you from having to introduce yourself individually.

Current coworkers

Finding things to talk about with your coworkers besides work can be difficult, especially if the only thing you have in common is the job itself. In this scenario it is important to take the time to look for hidden similarities that you might be able to then bond over. Barring that, consider the following conversation starters.

Ask how their day or week is going:

This is an especially useful tactic in this situation as everyone has some part of their job that they want to vent about, but few are able to do so appropriately. This will almost always give you an in while also allowing you to continue to look for similarities you might have at the same time. What's more, you might find that you had previously misjudged them and find that you actually just have similar personalities.

Match the time and place:

There are natural conversation starters built in to the work week, the start of the week is great for asking about the exciting things that happened last weekend; the middle of the week is great for complaining about how much work there is left to do; and the end of the week is great for talking about upcoming plans. Likewise, if you are trying to get to know a specific co-worker better, angle for a scenario that will force you to work or go someplace together so you can have an uninterrupted conversation.

Utilize differences:

If you can't seem to find common ground with a specific colleague, your best bet might instead be to head towards the differences instead of running away from them. If you are younger than your coworkers who have almost college age children, for example, you might have valuable insight into the process that they might appreciate because their references are all 2 decades or so farther out of date. Likewise, it might be a good opportunity for you to learn something that you otherwise never would. Start asking questions and you never know when you might discover a new passion just waiting to take over your life.

Chapter 10: Conversing on a Date

Finding things to talk about on a date can be tricky, especially when you are still feeling one another out. Luckily, there are a number of things that you can talk about to get things moving in the right direction before moving on to the tips discussed in the earlier chapters.

Talk about how awkward first dates can be:

If you come up against a lull in the conversation, this is one of the best times to comment on it because everyone knows that first dates are awkward, regardless of the circumstances leading up to them. This naturally makes it a great way to talk about something you have in common and admitting that it is awkward will often lead into stories of past dates that were really bad. This is ideal because it makes you look better than those other people by comparison while also making you both feel more comfortable.

Be familiar with current events:

One of the best ways to salvage a flagging first date conversation is to bring up current events. Happy or sad, it doesn't really matter as long as it is not politically charged and it is important enough (or cute enough) to stimulate conversation. It doesn't matter how interested you are in such things in general, the point is to get the conversation flowing so you can move on to areas of shared interest.

Don't be afraid to discuss what's going on in your day:

Unlike in many other instances, this is a time where simply talking about what has been going on in your life recently is acceptable, as long as there is still plenty of back and forth in the conversation. This is the sort of thing that you should be interested in finding out about the other person and ideally what they want to hear about from you. Only by sharing and asking about the little things will you be able to determine if you are truly compatible.

Ask the right open ended questions:

The best open ended questions to talk about while on a date are those that show you were paying attention the last time the two of you spoke recently. You want to go with something that is specific enough that they are likely to have a detailed response to while still general enough that the question can't be answered in just a few sentences.

Comment on appearance:

Be on the lookout for especially interesting accessories or pieces of clothing. Anything you see that appears as though the other person put special thought into wearing it for the occasion is something that warrants commenting on. This can also be a great way to find out more about the other person or hone in on additional hobbies or interest. Remember, an opened ended question is "I like that accessory or clothing item, it looks like it has a story behind it? A closed question, on the other hand, is "How long have you owned that accessory or clothing item?" It can be difficult to phrase questions properly in the moment at first, but it will get easier with practice.

Follow up:

While you are talking, keep track of particular information fragments that the other person mentions so that you can bring them up again when the conversation begins to lull. Not only will this show the other person that you are interested in them, it will show that you are a good listener as well. Following up will also help you to get to know the person you are on the date with on more than just a surface level.

Be realistic:

It is important to keep in mind that it is just a date and that if the conversation drops off from time to time it isn't the end of the world. Remember, being nervous won't help matters any and if it doesn't go well you never have discuss it again. With that being said, it is also important to remember that you simply can't connect with everyone and sometimes there is just going to be nothing to talk about. Don't beat yourself up in these situations, simply get through as best you can and hope for the best next time.

Conclusion

Thank for making it through to the end of *Small Talk: Master the Art of Small Talk Easily and Effectively with These 10 Easy Steps*; let's hope it was informative and able to provide you with all of the tools you need to achieve your goals both in the near term and for the months and years ahead. Remember, just because you've finished this book doesn't mean there is nothing left to learn on the topic. Becoming an expert at something is a marathon, not a sprint; slow and steady wins the race.

The next step is to stop reading and to start preparing yourself to have conversations with strangers. Don't forget, conversing easily is a skill which means that you will only improve with practice. The early going is likely to be rough, but forewarned is forearmed and being prepared for the awkwardness will make it more manageable. Always keep a reasonable level of expectations when it comes to your results and you will be talking to strangers with ease sooner than you might expect.

Finally, if you found this book useful in anyway, a review on Amazon is always appreciated!

Preview of "Living with Less" by Jessica Forrest

Discover the Joy of Less and Simplify your Life

What is Minimalism?

At the heart of western society there is an undercurrent of un-fulfillment. Every day we wake up, eat, wash, go to our jobs, come home, and make dinner and then go back to sleep. At some point along our lives we lost that sense of wonder and direction that we possessed when we were younger.

We go through the motions of our lives without being connected or immersed in what we are doing. As a result a myriad of different perspectives and philosophies have arisen by different thinkers in order to tell us what we are doing wrong and how we should fix it.

Some of us tell us we should travel and that our life is lackluster unless we are climbing mountains and constantly seeking new exotic challenges. Other views talk about the importance of success and aiming higher, climbing the business world and all of the hurdles it presents.

Minimalists look at the problem in a different way. The problem with our modern lifestyle is not that something is missing, it is the opposite; that we have far too much. We have so much stuff that we lose track of the few things that are important. We hound clutter – both physically and emotionally – until the things that make us happy are buried under everything else. As a result our lives lack that vitality and spark that makes life truly worth living.

On the same vein, for minimalists, the way to reignite your life and reclaim your happiness is not found on foreign shores or in achievements in the business world, it is realizing what in your life already makes you happy and changing your life to revolve around that.

Although minimalism is undoubtedly a movement and an idea with deep spiritual notions, don't make the mistake of thinking that all minimalists are hermits, monks or deeply religious. Minimalists are generally indistinguishable from anyone else in a crowd; they are people you know, people at your workplace and people with ordinary lives. All that is required to be minimalist is a simple change in your perspective.

To be precise, minimalists wage a peaceful war against clutter of all sorts. Regardless of whether we consider ourselves especially materialistic or not, an average person in the western world will grow to own a staggering amount of possessions throughout their lives.

From books, to games, to computers, laptops, phones, clothes, cars, dishes, cutlery, Christmas decorations, cleaning equipment, furniture novelties, and food, the amount of sheer 'stuff' a person collects is overwhelming. Yet, underneath all these items a truth remains dormant and forgotten; most of these items are not necessary and very few contribute to your happiness in any meaningful way.

Take a moment and ask yourself how many items in your life that you need and how many items actually give you genuine pleasure and contentment. Look at your bookshelves, stocked with hundreds of different books. How many have you actually read all the way through? How many do you actually require for constant use? Can you really say that any of these books change your life for the better? Would you notice if one of these books went missing?

Minimalists have asked themselves these types of questions and more regarding every possession they own. Moreover, minimalists have realized that in an honest and practical sense that most of their possessions are either completely unnecessary or do not make them happier – so they get rid of them.

In addition to the realization that the majority of their possessions do not actively contribute to their happiness, minimalists also recognize that keeping unnecessary items actually makes their life more difficult and unhappier.

A bookshelf full of unread books is an eyesore – it is a waste of space that could be left open, making your house feeling spacious and uplifting. It's also a chore in the sense that these books must be dusted and cleaned occasionally and must be organized and carefully arranged. If you do actually require a book for a specific reason it's not a simple task of just grabbing that book from where you made room for it.
Instead you must rummage and search through your amateur

library, wasting time and energy in the process. If you ever need to move or change the position of your furniture than moving that bookshelf is a huge challenge just by itself.

Of course these hassles are not a big problem by themselves, at least not in the case of a single bookshelf. However, when you have entire household stuffed to the brim of these pointless possessions these small efforts and hassles multiply exponentially. Simple tasks become difficult and so much of your life becomes dedicated and locked down just to looking after, maintaining and managing your possessions.

It becomes taxing and draining and redirects your time away from quality time with your friends and family as well as pursuing your passions. Every item is an item that must be cleaned or moved out the way when you are vacuuming or dusting.

They must be organized in complicated patterns just to make room for their presence and if you fail to constantly keep up, these items won't fit neatly in your cupboards and rooms. They get in your way when you are trying to find something you need, often finding that gadget or equipment is buried in the attic or behind a dozen other boxes with a bunch of junk in them – it's exhausting.

Therefore minimalists recognize that everything they don't frequently use or absolutely need is clutter and lowers the quality of their lives. By discarding, selling or gifting these items away, they give themselves more freedom, time and space to focus on what they actually want to do.

Although minimalists mostly concern themselves with unnecessary items, minimalists can also look at their responsibilities, duties and chores, eliminating unnecessary burdens from their life. Minimalists change their lives to make room and time for their activities they love; this might involve changing jobs or career, making a determined effort to manage their money and debt to give them financial control over their time.

Minimalists aren't locked into their 9-5 office job because they need money for the loan they took out for their car and they don't chain themselves down with large mortgages that dictate their life for the next 20 years.

Likewise minimalists don't go to un-enjoyable social gatherings out of obligation or constantly bow down to what other people expect of them. Instead they go to gatherings if they make them happy and forge their own path. This guide will mostly focus on the physical aspect of minimalism but please bear in mind the other ways in which minimalism can change your life.

Finally, minimalism also relates to an artistic movement that arose in the 1960's. In the previous decades, art had focused on being flamboyant, decorative and detailed, so much so that certain artists felt overloaded. These artists started to focus on what they felt were essential and most important aspects of any particular piece of art – the lines, the shapes, the colors and the ideas.

As a result minimalist art and minimalist inspired decoration have an easily distinguishable stripped-down and bear aesthetic. In a sense by removing excess detail and visual stimulation, the remaining section become more important and more purposeful. Instead of your eyes becoming bombarded by different intricacies, you can instead direction your attention to the individual components in the art, or even the piece in entirety. There is a simple pleasure in being absorbed in a piece of art, allowing you attention to deepen and sink into the piece.

Minimalist art lead to minimalist design, which is popular for many individuals with busy and stressful lives, to help them relax, and be more productive. If your environment is serene and calm, it helps you become serene and calm by extension. This doesn't mean that your décor is devoid of any decoration or ornaments, just that they are well-considered and sparse. A colorful vase can bring life to an otherwise empty room and a piece of artwork can energize a blank wall.

Printed in Great Britain
by Amazon